For The Matterhorn's Sake, Zermatt Is The Place!

A Kid's Guide To Zermatt, Switzerland

PHOTOGRAPHY BY JOHN D. WEIGAND
POETRY BY PENELOPE DYAN

Bellissima Publishing, LLC
Jamul, California
www.bellissimapublishing.com

ISBN 978-1-935630-04-3

First Edition

For Kids Who Love To Imagine
And For Parents Who Love
To Imagine With Them!

For The Matterhorn's Face, Zermatt Is The Place!

Bellissima Publishing, LLC

Introduction

The mountain village of Zermatt, Switzerland is nestled in a valley between steep mountains, and it is dominated by the Matterhorn. When you exit your Swiss-red train, and see the cobblestone streets and horses and carriages, you immediately will notice are no cars. The air is clean and fresh, and the people want to keep it that way! The main street bustles with people shopping, dining and having a good time, and there are no tour busses anywhere. In short, everything is cute and fun, and you immediately know where Walt Disney got many of his ideas for Disneyland, as you can see the Matterhorn from nearly every prospective in the Zermatt village. And this is exactly why photographer John D. Weigand and author and poet Penelope Dyan went there, to capture some of the magic of Zermatt. It seemed like the perfect spot for kids, nestled in the serenity of the Swiss Alps. . . just waiting to be ogled and explored.

The Zermatt nights were even more beautiful than the day as the Weigand photographs portray, but most amazing of all was the Matterhorn, shining white against the sky by day, and full of amazing color by night.

For The Matterhorn's Face, Zermatt Is The Place!

Bellissima Publishing, LLC

For The Matterhorn's Face, Zermatt Is The Place!

A Kid's Guide To Zermatt, Switzerland

PHOTOGRAPHY BY JOHN D. WEIGAND
POETRY BY PENELOPE DYAN

When you go to downtown Zermatt,
You will know EXACTLY where you're at!
You can get aboard the Matterhorn Swiss red train at Visp,
where the air is blue and cool and crisp.
You will travel partly by regular rail and partly by cog,
You can write all about it in your travel journey's log.

In Zermatt there are lots of shops and places to eat, where you can find food that is tasty and sweet.

To work up an appetite you can ski!
That is what I would do if it was up to me.

Or maybe you would like to play some ball.
Because you ARE on vacation, after all!

And the bratwurst and bread is really great.
I know that for sure, because THAT's what I ATE!

And the chocolate in Switzerland is really like no other.
Buy a piece for yourself, and get some for your mother!

You can see a carriage with horses at the trot.
You can see an awfully lot.

See the hills of Zermatt covered in snow,
a winter wonderland, a beautiful place to go!

And from our hotel room going right up to the sky. . .
(I thought that I could touch it if I wanted to try)
Was the beautiful Matterhorn majestic and white. . .
And the sun shown down on it ever so bright.

You can have some great apple strudel. . .

at the Cafe Du Pont. . . and what's more. . .
You can by souvenirs, at a souvenir store!
And when you eat the apple strudel you will note every bite,
Is sweet and flaky and a sheer delight.

rivella

Bratwurst
mit Brot
und Sauce 7.-
* * *

**CAFE
DU PONT**
Walliserspezialitäten

HENNIEZ

Menu 1
Bouillon Maison
Bratwurst mit Rösti
und Salat 22.9fr.
Menu 2.
Paniertes Schnitzel
(Poulet) mit Pommes
Frites und Salat 22.9fr.

Wurstsalat
garniert
16.Fr.

CARDINAL

div. Fondue
Raclette
Walliser
Teller
Schnecken
Käseschnitte

Fondue Pro Person
Fondue normal Pro Person 22.9fr.
Fondue mit Kräutern 23.9fr.
Fondue mit Tomaten 23.9fr.
Fondue mit Steinpilzen 23.9fr.
Alle Fondue mit Brot u.
Kartoffeln
Hobel - Käse Pro Person 6.9fr.
Wurstsalat garniert 16.-
Raclette 8.9fr.

As the sun sets on the Matterhorn and you're ready for bed,
to your comfortable hotel room you will then head.

And on the hills above you the houses lit bright. . .
look so warm and comforting in the cold, dark night.

If you feel hungry on the way back to your hotel.
there is a place you can eat that has a name you know well!
You can go to McDonald's for dinner or for just a snack,
or to the Du Pont Cafe you can ALWAYS go back!

You can take a cog train up to the top of the hill,
You can get off at Gonergrat (or before)
and ski, or do what you will.
You can just get right out of the train, and then. . .
put on your skis and ski down and then ride up again.

There are two observatories at Gonergrat, Switzerland,
(at over ten thousand feet)
And and if you are hungry after the cog wheel train ride. . .
You can get something to eat!
The Matterhorn stands ANOTHER four thousand feet high,
And you can look at it out the restaurant window
as you eat french fries and pie!

And when you return and go back down the hill,
there stands the Matterhorn silent and still.

Then all of a sudden you see a tree!
It looks taller than the Matterhorn and that simply CAN'T be!
Now which thing do you think is taller, and do YOU know why?
Are we seeing an illusion as we look toward the sky?

Here is a building with a roof made of stone slate.
It is like stepping into the past, and everything's great!

And when you go home and are sleeping in your own bed. . .
the nights of Zermatt will dance in the dreams in your head.

And you will remember the little church,
you saw from the train window, in the snow,
and remember that next time that here is where you will go.
From the top of the mountains to the valley below. . .
You will remember Zermatt, Switzerland
and the newly fallen snow!
But the Matterhorn, the REAL Matterhorn
is what you will really remember,
And you will hope you can see it again
BEFORE school starts in September.
From the top of your head to the tip of your toes,
right down to the snow that fell on your nose,
YOU will remember THIS adventure as being out of sight!
AND how you saw the Matterhorn by day and by night!

Lightning Source UK Ltd.
Milton Keynes UK
UKHW051042071222
413452UK00002B/95